TO MY BODY WITH LOVE

TO MY BODY WITH LOVE

CHANELLE FLEARY

To My Body With Love

All rights reserved
Copyright © 2023 by Chanelle Fleary

No part of this publication may be reproduced, distributed, or transmitted in any form or by any means, including photocopying, recording, or other electronic or mechanical methods, without the prior written permission of the publisher, except in the case of brief quotations embodied in critical reviews and certain other noncommercial uses permitted by copyright law.

Published by BooxAI
ISBN: 978-965-578-660-6

CONTENTS

PREFACE

In a society that frequently expects flawlessness and nurtures self-questioning, it is all too easy to forget the beauty and power that resides within our own bodies. We are bombarded with images of airbrushed models, social media influencers with seemingly flawless physiques, and societal expectations that dictate what we should look like. In this relentless pursuit of an idealized image, we often neglect the one vessel that carries us through life—the very embodiment of our existence: our bodies.

"To My Body With Love" is an intimate exploration, a heartfelt ode to the remarkable and resilient nature of the human body. It is a gentle reminder to appreciate and honor the intricate tapestry of muscles, bones, and organs that enable us to experience the world in all its splendor. This collection of words seeks to inspire a renewed sense of self-love, acceptance, and gratitude for the remarkable vessel that houses our dreams, desires, and emotions.

Within these pages, you will find a mosaic of personal reflections, empowering affirmations, and gentle reminders that invite you to embrace your body as a cherished companion and steadfast ally. It is a celebration of all body types, shapes, and sizes, emphasizing the inherent worth and intrinsic beauty that each one possesses. Through poignant prose and tender verses, "To My Body With Love" aims to dismantle the harmful narratives that plague our relationship with ourselves and encourages a shift towards a more compassionate and nurturing connection.

In a world that often teaches us to criticize and judge our own bodies, it is time to rewrite the narrative. It is time to replace self-loathing with self-acceptance, comparison with appreciation, and doubt with reverence. "To My Body With Love" serves as a gentle guide, offering solace and support as you embark on a journey of self-discovery, self-compassion, and healing.

May these words serve as a beacon of light, illuminating the path towards a deeper understanding of your own unique beauty and worth. May they remind you that your body is not an object to be scrutinized or belittled, but a vessel of strength, resilience, and limitless potential. May they inspire you to shower your body with tenderness, kindness, and love.

With each turn of the page, may you find solace, inspiration, and the gentle reminder that you are worthy of love, exactly as you are.

With love,

Chanelle A. Fleary

INTRODUCTION: EMBRACING SELF-LOVE AND BODY POSITIVITY

In a world that often emphasizes unrealistic beauty standards and places immense pressure on individuals to conform to a certain image, the importance of self-love and body positivity cannot be overstated. Embracing these concepts allows us to break free from the chains of comparison, self-doubt, and negative self-perception, and instead fosters a deep sense of acceptance, appreciation, and empowerment.

Self-love, at its core, is the act of caring for oneself unconditionally, both physically and emotionally. It involves recognizing and valuing our own worth, acknowledging our strengths and weaknesses, and treating ourselves with kindness and compassion. Self-love is not selfish or narcissistic; rather, it is a fundamental prerequisite for leading a fulfilling and balanced life. Body positivity, on the other hand, is a movement that challenges society's narrow definition of beauty and promotes inclusivity and acceptance of all body types, shapes, and sizes. It encourages us to celebrate diversity and recognize that beauty exists in infinite forms. Body positivity urges us to reject harmful societal norms that perpetuate body shaming, unrealistic expectations, and harmful comparisons, and instead embrace body acceptance, self-care, and self-expression.

The journey towards self-love and body positivity is not always easy. It requires unlearning deeply ingrained societal beliefs, overcoming personal insecurities, and challenging our own negative self-talk. It involves shifting our focus from external validation to internal fulfillment, from seeking perfection to embracing our authentic selves.

However, the rewards of embracing self-love and body positivity are immense. When we learn to love and accept ourselves, flaws and all, we experience increased confidence, improved mental well-being, and enhanced overall happiness. We become less susceptible to the judgments and opinions of others, and instead develop a strong sense of self-worth that radiates from within.

Furthermore, embracing self-love and body positivity creates a ripple effect that extends beyond ourselves. By embracing our own unique beauty and worth, we inspire those around us to do the same. We become agents of change, challenging societal norms and paving the way for a more inclusive and accepting world.

In this exploration of self-love and body positivity, we will delve into various aspects of these concepts, offering insights, tips, and practical strategies to help foster a positive relationship with ourselves and our bodies. We will address issues such as overcoming body shame, cultivating self-compassion, nurturing a healthy body image, and embracing self-care practices that promote well-being.

Together, let us embark on this transformative journey towards self-love and body positivity, where we can learn to appreciate our bodies as unique vessels of our experiences, and celebrate the beauty that resides within each and every one of us.

To My Body With Love

Today and every day, I choose to embrace you with boundless gratitude and unconditional love. You are a magnificent vessel that carries me through life's journey, and I am eternally grateful for your strength, resilience, and unwavering support.

With each breath, you give me the precious energy to pursue my dreams, to embrace joy, and to conquer challenges. You are a masterpiece, flawlessly crafted with intricacies and complexities that make you uniquely mine. From the tips of my toes to the crown of my head, you are a remarkable work of art.

I promise to nurture you, to treat you with kindness and respect, and to listen attentively to your whispers and needs. I acknowledge that you are ever-evolving, and I promise to honor your growth and transformation, both physically and emotionally.

In a world that often tries to dictate standards of beauty and perfection, I declare that you are already perfect as you are. Your curves, lines, and imperfections tell stories of resilience, laughter, and love. You are a testament to my existence and the embodiment of my journey.

Today, I release any negative thoughts or judgments I may have held against you. I replace them with words of compassion, acceptance, and love. I vow to celebrate your uniqueness and cherish all that you do for me.

To my body, I say thank you. Thank you for allowing me to experience the wonders of this world, for dancing, for embracing my loved ones, and for providing a home for my soul. With love and gratitude, I promise to nourish and treasure you, always.

Forever yours,

MEDITATION

Take a moment to find a comfortable position, sitting or lying down, allowing your body to settle into a state of relaxation. Close your eyes gently and bring your attention to your breath. Notice the gentle rise and fall of your chest with each inhale and exhale. Take a few deep breaths, breathing in slowly through your nose, and exhaling fully through your mouth.

As you continue to breathe, bring your awareness to the present moment and the intention of cultivating love and compassion for your body. Allow any tension or stress to melt away with each breath, creating space for self-care and acceptance.

Now, envision yourself surrounded by warm, soothing light. Feel this radiant light enveloping your entire being, embracing you with unconditional love and support. Let this light symbolize the love and appreciation you deserve.

With each breath, extend this love and gratitude towards your body. Visualize each part of your body, starting with your toes and gradually moving up to your head. As you focus on each area, send thoughts of love, kindness, and gratitude.

Reflect on the incredible abilities of your body. Think of the times it has carried you through challenging moments, healed itself, and provided you with the experiences that have shaped your journey. Acknowledge its resilience and strength.

As you continue to breathe, repeat the following affirmations silently or out loud:

"To my body, I offer love and acceptance. I honor and cherish you."

"I am grateful for the vessel that carries me through life's adventures."

"I appreciate the unique beauty and strength of my body."

"I nurture and care for my body with compassion and kindness."

Take a few more moments to connect with the sensations in your body. Notice any areas that may need extra love and attention. Send healing energy to those places, allowing yourself to feel a sense of comfort and relief.

When you feel ready, gently bring your attention back to your breath. Take a few moments to sit with the feelings of love and gratitude you have cultivated for your body. Know that you can return to this space of self-love and appreciation whenever you need it.

When you are ready, slowly open your eyes, carrying this sense of love and appreciation with you as you embark on the journey of reading "To My Body With Love."

1

GRATITUDE FOR MY BODY

"**G**ratitude for my body is the nourishing embrace of self-love, a celebration of the vessel that carries my spirit through this beautiful journey called life. In its strength, in its imperfections, I find a profound appreciation for the miraculous gift of existence." - Chanelle Fleary

Within the pages of this enlightening chapter, we shall embark on a profound exploration of the concept of gratitude for our bodies. Our bodies, undeniably marvelous and intricately orchestrated vessels, serve as the conduits through which we experience the multifaceted beauty of life. It is of paramount importance to acknowledge and cherish the awe-inspiring capabilities and harmonious functions that our bodies possess. By wholeheartedly cultivating gratitude for our bodies, we have the power to forge a profoundly positive and enriching relationship with ourselves.

Throughout the course of this chapter, we will embark on a captivating journey, unearthing the various aspects of our bodies that deserve our unwavering gratitude. From the majesty of our senses, allowing us to behold breathtaking sights, savor the delectable flavors, embrace the tender warmth of touch, and revel in the symphony of sounds, to the intricate marvels of our internal systems, seamlessly coordinating countless processes to sustain our existence, our bodies are a wondrous tapestry of miracles.

Moreover, this chapter will serve as an invaluable guide, offering practical suggestions and insightful strategies for embracing and practicing gratitude for our bodies. Through mindful awareness, deliberate reflection, and intentional acts of appreciation, we can unlock the transformative power of gratitude, nurturing a deep sense of connection, acceptance, and love for our physical selves.

By fostering gratitude for our bodies, we not only honor the remarkable vessel that carries us through life but also cultivate a profound sense of self-worth, acceptance, and compassion. This chapter will empower us to embark on a personal odyssey, uncovering the myriad reasons why our bodies deserve our unwavering appreciation.

So, let us embark on this enlightening expedition, embracing the wonders of our bodies, and enriching our lives through the transformative practice of gratitude. Together, we will embark on a path of self-discovery, unlocking the boundless potential for joy, contentment, and holistic well-being that lies within the realm of appreciating our remarkable bodies.

Reflecting in the Mirror on Gratitude for My Body

As I stand in front of my mirror, enveloped by the stillness of the room, I take a deliberate, deep breath. With a sense of anticipation, I cast my gaze upon the reflective surface, prepared to confront the image that stares back at me. What I see is a woman no longer looking like she once did. This woman before me is full-figured, her body tracing the contours of a life well-lived. The passage of time has etched its mark upon her, leaving behind a tapestry of experiences that have shaped her into who she is today. The remnants of age, the indelible imprints of motherhood, the battles fought against illness, and the myriad trials and triumphs of existence—all have left their fingerprints on her physical form. Yet, as I continue to peer into the mirror, a profound shift occurs within me. Instead of lamenting the changes that time has wrought, I choose to embrace them. I choose to acknowledge the wisdom that resides within me, the resilience forged through hardships endured, and the love that has blossomed and flourished within the depths of my heart. In this moment, gratitude begins to unfurl within me like delicate tendrils reaching toward the sun. I am grateful for the body that has carried me through the labyrinth of life, for every scar that tells a story of survival, and for the moments of sheer joy and boundless laughter that have woven themselves into the fabric of my being.

With each passing second, I find myself enveloped in a profound sense of appreciation and self-love. No, I may not resemble the airbrushed images of supermodels that grace glossy magazine covers. I may not be a household name or possess the fame of a celebrity. But that is inconsequential, for I am me—Chanelle A. Fleary—and within the depths of my soul, I have discovered a love that transcends physical appearance. I have fallen deeply in love with the reflection before me, with the woman who has weathered storms and emerged stronger, with a soul that radiates authenticity and grace. In this sacred union of self-acceptance, I find solace and empowerment. I am a testament to the beauty found in resilience, the strength inherent in embracing one's true essence, and the unwavering power of self-love.

So, as I stand here, bathed in the gentle glow of self-compassion, I revel in the truth of who I am. I am a masterpiece in progress, a mosaic of imperfections woven together with threads of courage and resilience. And I am grateful—for the journey that has brought me here, for the woman I have become, and for the boundless love I have discovered for myself in the reflection of the mirror.

Exercise: Reflecting in the Mirror on Gratitude for My Body

Duration: 10-15 minutes

Materials needed: A mirror, a comfortable space

Instructions:

1. Find a quiet and comfortable space where you can have some privacy. Make sure you have access to a mirror, preferably a full-length mirror.

2. Stand in front of the mirror and take a few deep breaths to center yourself. Allow yourself to relax and let go of any tension in your body.

3. Begin by looking at your reflection without judgment or criticism. Simply observe your body from head to toe. Notice the shape, the curves, and the unique features that make you who you are. Remember that this exercise is about cultivating gratitude and appreciation for your body.

4. Take a moment to focus on your breath and bring your attention to your heart center. Close your eyes if it feels comfortable, and think about all the amazing things your body allows you to do on a daily basis. Consider the different functions and abilities your body has, such as breathing, moving, seeing, hearing, and feeling.

5. Open your eyes and continue to gaze at yourself in the mirror. Start by expressing gratitude for your physical health. Acknowledge the strength and resilience of your body, which enables you to pursue your passions and live a fulfilling life.

6. Shift your focus to specific body parts. Begin at your feet and work your way up. As you look at each body part, express gratitude for its unique role and function. Appreciate your legs for carrying you throughout the day, your arms for their strength and ability, your hands for their dexterity, and so on.

7. Now, think about all the experiences your body has allowed you to have. Consider the places you've been, the activities you've enjoyed, and the relationships you've formed—all made possible by your physical body. Express gratitude for the senses that allow you to experience the world around you.

8. Take a moment to send love and appreciation to your body. Visualize a warm, golden light enveloping your entire being, nourishing and cherishing every cell. Feel the love and gratitude radiating from within you and extending outwards.

9. Before concluding the exercise, take a final look at yourself in the mirror. Smile and affirm your gratitude for your body, saying something like, "Thank you, body, for all that you do. I appreciate and love you just as you are."

10. Take a deep breath, slowly release it, and gently step away from the mirror. Allow the feelings of gratitude and appreciation to linger within you as you continue with your day.

Remember, this exercise is meant to foster a positive and loving relationship with your body. Practice it regularly to cultivate a deeper sense of gratitude and acceptance for all the incredible things your body does for you.

1.1 Recognizing the Gift of Life

Life is an extraordinary gift that we often take for granted. In the hustle and bustle of our daily lives, it's easy to lose sight of the sheer miracle of existence. Recognizing the gift of life means acknowledging and appreciating the precious opportunity we have been given to experience the world. Every breath we take, every beat of our heart, and every sensation we feel are reminders of the incredible blessing it is to be alive. We are part of an intricate web of life, connected to the vastness of the universe. Taking a moment to pause and reflect on this interconnectedness can fill us with a sense of wonder, gratitude, and humility. When we recognize the gift of life, we become more mindful of the beauty that surrounds us. The vibrant colors of nature, the laughter of loved ones, and the simple pleasures of everyday life take on a deeper significance. We begin to savor each moment, knowing that time is fleeting and that every experience holds unique value. As we continue to recognize the gift of life, we also gain perspective. We become aware of the transient nature of existence, and this awareness can inspire us to live with greater purpose and intention. We start to focus on what truly matters: nurturing relationships, pursuing our passions, and making a positive difference in the world.

As I engage in deep introspection regarding my existence within the vast expanse of this world, my thoughts gravitate towards a profound reflection on the timeless wisdom encapsulated in the sacred pages of the Holy Bible. Specifically, I am drawn to the powerful words articulated in Jeremiah 1:5, as beautifully conveyed in the King James Version. This verse resounds with a divine revelation, a revelation that transcends the boundaries of time and space. It affirms that even before the intricate process of my physical formation took place within the nurturing sanctuary of a mother's womb, I was already known by the Creator Himself. In that preconceived realm, where the tapestry of life began to take shape, I was set apart and sanctified by the divine hand. In the grand tapestry of existence, I find solace and awe in realizing that my purpose transcends the mere boundaries of my mortal existence. I am called to be a beacon of light, a conduit of divine wisdom, and a messenger of hope to all nations. It is as if the very fabric of reality was woven with a thread of destiny, and I have been ordained by God to fulfill a prophetic role in the unfolding story of humanity.

The weight of this realization is humbling, for it reminds me that my presence in this life is not a mere coincidence, but a deliberate act of divine orchestration. It instills within me a profound sense of gratitude, an overwhelming appreciation for the gift of life that has been bestowed upon me. How can I not be grateful for the privilege of existing, for the opportunity to witness the beauty of creation, and for the chance to make a positive impact on the lives of others?

As I navigate the ebb and flow of existence, I find solace in the knowledge that I am not alone. For every step I take, every decision I make, and every challenge I face, I am guided by the hands of an omnipotent and loving Creator. It is this assurance that sustains me in times of uncertainty, strengthens me in times of adversity, and fills my heart with an unyielding hope that transcends the limitations of mortality. In conclusion, the profound words of Jeremiah 1:5 serve as a timeless reminder of the divine purpose imbued within each and every one of us. They beckon us to embrace our unique calling, to recognize the sanctity of our existence, and to express our gratitude for the precious gift of life. May we all find solace, inspiration, and a renewed sense of purpose as we embark on this remarkable journey of being.

Exercise: Gratitude Journaling

Objective: To cultivate a sense of gratitude and recognize the gift of life through journaling.

Instructions:

1. Find a quiet and comfortable place where you can focus on your thoughts without distractions.

2. Take a few deep breaths to center yourself and bring your attention to the present moment.

3. Take a moment to reflect on your life and the various aspects that you are grateful for. Consider the following categories:

- *Personal relationships:* Think about the people in your life who bring you joy, love, and support. It could be family members, friends, partners, or mentors.

- *Health and well-being:* Reflect on the physical and mental aspects of your health that you appreciate. Consider the abilities and strengths of your body and mind.

- *Accomplishments and experiences:* Recall the achievements, milestones, and positive experiences that have shaped your life. It could be personal growth, professional successes, or memorable moments.

- *Nature and the world around you:* Contemplate the beauty of nature, the environment, and the world we live in. Think about the simple pleasures nature provides.

- *Opportunities and privileges:* Acknowledge the opportunities and privileges that have come your way, such as education, access to resources, or a safe and stable environment.

4. Take out a journal or a piece of paper and write down at least five things you are grateful for in each of the categories mentioned above. Be as specific as possible and try to connect with the emotions associated with your gratitude.

5. After completing your gratitude journal, take a moment to read through what you have written. Allow yourself to fully embrace the feelings of gratitude and appreciation.

6. Whenever you feel down or in need of a reminder of the gift of life, revisit your gratitude journal. It can serve as a source of inspiration and a reminder of the positive aspects of your life.

1.2 Cultivating Appreciation for Physical Abilities

Our physical abilities are an incredible asset that allows us to interact with the world and fulfill our desires and aspirations. From the simplest tasks to the most complex endeavors, our bodies enable us to experience life to its fullest. Cultivating appreciation for our physical abilities means recognizing and valuing the remarkable capabilities that our bodies possess. Consider the mechanisms of the human body—the strength of our muscles, the flexibility of our joints, and the coordination of our movements. These abilities allow us to navigate the world, engage in physical activities, and express ourselves in various ways. Whether it's dancing, playing a sport, or simply hugging a loved one, our physical abilities enhance our experiences and bring us joy.

Appreciating our physical abilities also involves taking care of our bodies. Engaging in regular exercise, maintaining a balanced diet, and getting sufficient rest are essential for preserving and optimizing our physical well-being. When we treat our bodies with kindness and respect, we honor the incredible vessel that carries us through life. Cultivating an appreciation for our physical abilities goes beyond recognizing the external manifestations of our bodies. It involves embracing our uniqueness and accepting ourselves as we are. Each body is different, and comparison to others only diminishes our own worth. By appreciating our own physical abilities, we can cultivate self-love and develop a positive body image.

Exercise: Mindful Movement and Meditation

Objective: The objective of this exercise is to cultivate appreciation for your physical abilities and develop a deeper connection with your body through mindfulness movement and meditation.

Instructions:

1. Find a quiet and comfortable space where you can move freely without distractions. You can choose to do this exercise indoors or outdoors, depending on your preference.

2. Begin by standing tall with your feet shoulder-width apart. Close your eyes and take a few deep breaths to center yourself and bring your attention to the present moment.

3. Start gently moving your body, allowing your movements to be slow, deliberate, and mindful. Let go of any tension or stiffness in your muscles.

4. Begin by focusing on your feet. Slowly lift one foot off the ground and feel the sensation of balance and stability as your weight shifts to the other foot. Notice the intricate sensations in your feet—the warmth, the texture of the ground beneath them, and any other sensations that arise.

5. Gradually move your attention upward through your body, paying attention to each body part as you go. Move deliberately, exploring the range of motion in your joints, the strength in your muscles, and the sensations that arise.

6. As you move, bring your awareness to the different physical abilities that you possess. Notice the strength in your legs that allows you to walk, run, or dance. Appreciate the flexibility in your spine that enables you to bend, twist, and reach. Acknowledge the dexterity in your hands that allows you to create, touch, and feel. Recognize the capacity of your lungs as you breathe deeply and nourish your body.

7. As you continue to move, let go of any judgments or comparisons. This exercise is not about achieving a particular level of physical ability but rather about appreciating what your body can do in this present moment.

8. If your mind starts to wander or you become distracted, gently bring your attention back to the sensations in your body and the movements you are making. Embrace a mindset of curiosity and exploration.

9. Continue mindfulness movement meditation for as long as it feels comfortable to you. You can explore different movements, such as stretching, twisting, reaching, or even dancing. Allow yourself to truly appreciate and celebrate the physical abilities you possess.

10. After you have finished the exercise, take a moment to reflect on the experience. Notice any changes in your mindset or your perception of your physical abilities. Consider how cultivating appreciation for your body can positively impact your overall well-being.

1.3 Honoring the Strength and Resilience of My Body

Our bodies possess an innate strength and resilience that allows us to overcome challenges and adapt to various circumstances. From healing wounds to withstanding stress, our bodies continually demonstrate their remarkable capacity to endure and recover. Honoring the strength and resilience of our bodies means acknowledging and respecting these qualities. Think about the times when your body has carried you through difficult situations—times when you pushed through physical exhaustion, recovered from illness or injury, or coped with emotional stress. Our bodies have the incredible ability to bounce back and restore balance. By recognizing and honoring this resilience, we gain a renewed sense of appreciation for our bodies' capabilities. Honoring the strength and resilience of our bodies also involves developing a compassionate relationship with ourselves. It means treating our bodies with kindness and care, listening to their needs, and responding with love and compassion. This includes practicing self-care, setting healthy boundaries, and prioritizing rest and relaxation.

When we honor the strength and resilience of our bodies, we also recognize the importance of maintaining a positive mindset. Our thoughts and beliefs have a profound impact on our well-being. By cultivating self-compassion, practicing gratitude, and embracing a positive outlook, we can support our bodies in their journey towards health and vitality. Furthermore, honoring the strength and resilience of our bodies involves celebrating our achievements and milestones, no matter how big or small. Each step forward, each accomplishment, and each moment of progress is a testament to the power within us. By acknowledging and celebrating these victories, we cultivate a sense of pride and confidence in our bodies' abilities. Finally, honoring the strength and resilience of our bodies means rejecting societal pressures and unrealistic standards. We live in a world that often imposes narrow definitions of beauty and success. However, true strength and resilience come in all shapes, sizes, and forms. Embracing our unique qualities and appreciating the diversity of bodies around us is a powerful act of self-acceptance and empowerment.

In conclusion, recognizing the gift of life, cultivating an appreciation for our physical abilities, and honoring the strength and resilience of our bodies are interconnected practices that can bring profound joy, gratitude, and self-love into our lives. By embracing these perspectives, we can develop a deeper connection with ourselves and the world around us, leading to a more fulfilling and meaningful existence.

Exercise: Embracing Body Appreciation

Duration: 30 minutes

Materials needed: Comfortable clothing, a yoga mat (optional)

Instructions:

1. Begin by finding a quiet and peaceful space where you can focus on yourself and your body. This could be a room in your house, a quiet spot in nature, or anywhere that makes you feel comfortable.

2. Sit or lie down in a comfortable position. Take a few deep breaths to center yourself and bring your attention to the present moment.

3. Close your eyes and reflect on the incredible strength and resilience of your body. Think about all the ways your body has supported you throughout your life and allowed you to experience the world. Acknowledge any challenges or hardships your body has faced and overcome.

4. Slowly begin to move your body in a way that feels good to you. This could be gentle stretches, yoga poses, or any other form of movement that

you enjoy. Focus on the sensations in your body and how each movement feels.

5. As you move, repeat positive affirmations or statements about your body. For example, you could say, "I am grateful for my body and all that it can do," or "I honor the strength and resilience of my body." Let these affirmations sink into your mind, and truly believe them.

6. Take your time and explore different movements and poses. Listen to your body and do what feels comfortable and empowering for you. If you feel any pain or discomfort, modify the movements or choose different ones that suit your body.

7. If you have a yoga mat, you can use it for additional comfort and support. However, this exercise can also be done without one.

8. Continue moving and affirming your body for at least 20 minutes, allowing positive energy to flow through you.

9. After the movement session, slowly come to a seated or lying position and take a few moments to rest and relax. Breathe deeply and express gratitude for your body and all that it does for you.

10. When you feel ready, gently open your eyes and take a moment to appreciate the experience. Reflect on how you feel after honoring the strength and resilience of your body.

2

ACCEPTING IMPERFECTIONS

"Embrace beauty in imperfection, for it is through our flaws that we find our true selves and the courage to grow."

In this pivotal moment in your life, it is imperative to wholeheartedly embrace the essence of your true self, regardless of the winding path you have traversed. Each step you have taken, each experience you have encountered, has shaped and molded you into the unique individual you are today. It is now time to shed the layers of self-doubt, societal expectations, and external influences that have veiled your true identity. Embracing your authentic self is an act of self-love and self-acceptance. It requires acknowledging and honoring your genuine desires, passions, and values. It means embracing your strengths and weaknesses, your quirks and idiosyncrasies, without judgment or shame. By recognizing and celebrating your own uniqueness, you open the door to a life of authenticity, fulfillment, and genuine connections. The journey towards self-acceptance may not always be smooth or straightforward. There may be moments of doubt, fear, and societal pressure pushing you towards conformity. However, true liberation lies in boldly embracing who you are, unapologetically and without compromise. When you align your thoughts, actions, and choices with your true self, you create a harmonious and empowering existence. Remember, you are the author of your own narrative. You have the power to rewrite your story, to cast aside the limitations imposed by others, and to embrace the truth that resides within you. Embracing your true self is an act of courage, resilience, and authenticity. It is an invitation to live a life that reflects your innermost desires, passions, and values.

Surround yourself with a supportive and nurturing community that celebrates and uplifts your true self. Seek out individuals who appreciate your unique qualities and encourage your growth. Engage in activities that bring you joy and allow your authentic self to shine brightly.

Embracing your true self is a lifelong journey, one that requires ongoing self-reflection, self-compassion, and self-discovery. It is a continuous process of unraveling the layers of conditioning and societal expectations, and reconnecting with the core of your being. Through this process, you will find liberation, fulfillment, and a profound sense of belonging. Now is the time to embark on this transformative journey. Embrace your authentic self, for you are deserving of love, acceptance, and the freedom to live a life that resonates with your true essence. Embrace the beauty and power that lies within you, and let it radiate through every aspect of your existence. The world awaits your unique contribution, and by embracing your true self, you will inspire others to do the same.

Exercise: Embracing Imperfections

Objective: To develop self-acceptance and cultivate a positive relationship with your body by embracing its imperfections.

Duration: 20-30 minutes

Materials needed:

- A quiet and comfortable space

- Pen and paper or a journal

- Optional: soothing background music

Instructions:

1. Find a quiet and comfortable space where you can relax and focus on yourself without distractions. You may choose to play some soothing background music to create a calming atmosphere.

2. Take a few deep breaths to center yourself and bring your attention to the present moment. Allow any tension or stress to melt away as you focus on your breath.

3. Take a moment to reflect on your body and its imperfections. Consider the areas or aspects of your body that you often criticize or feel insecure about. Acknowledge that imperfections are a natural part of being human and that everyone has them in some form or another.

4. Grab your pen and paper or journal and start writing a letter to your body. Begin by addressing it with love and gratitude. For example, you can start with, "Dear Body, I want to express my love and appreciation for everything you do for me."

5. Now, shift your focus to the imperfections you identified earlier. Write about each imperfection individually, acknowledging its presence and expressing acceptance and love for that part of your body. For example, if you are insecure about a scar, you might write, "Dear scar, I want to thank you for being a part of my story. You remind me of the experiences I have lived and the strength I possess."

6. As you write, try to shift your perspective from criticism to compassion. Emphasize the positive aspects or functions associated with each imperfection. Find beauty in the uniqueness and strength that these imperfections represent.

7. Once you have addressed each imperfection, take a moment to read your letter aloud. Hear the words of acceptance and love as they resonate in the space around you. Allow positive energy to fill your being.

8. Take a deep breath and let go of any remaining judgments or negative emotions associated with your body. Visualize those feelings being released and replaced with a sense of self-acceptance and love.

9. Close the exercise by expressing gratitude to yourself for taking this important step toward accepting your body's imperfections. Recognize that self-love and acceptance are ongoing journeys and commit to nurturing a positive relationship with your body going forward.

Remember, the purpose of this exercise is to embrace your body's imperfections and foster a sense of self-acceptance and love. Be patient and kind to yourself throughout the process.

2.1 Letting Go of Unrealistic Standards

In a world that frequently emphasizes perfection, releasing ourselves from unrealistic standards can be a significant challenge. The media bombards us with images of flawless individuals, creating the illusion that perfection is not only attainable but also necessary for happiness. However, striving for perfection can be exhausting and detrimental to our overall well-being. To truly embrace imperfections, it is crucial to confront and challenge these unrealistic standards. First and foremost, we must understand that perfection is merely an illusion. No one is flawless, and we all have our fair share of flaws. Instead of striving for an unattainable ideal, we should embrace the idea that our imperfections are what make us unique and human. True beauty lies in authenticity rather than conforming to some unrealistic image.

To break free from these standards, we need to question their sources. Reflect on the influence of the media, societal expectations, and personal beliefs. Recognize that these standards are often impossible to meet and can result in feelings of inadequacy. Instead, redirect your focus towards setting realistic goals and expectations for yourself. Accept that you are a work in progress, and growth is more important than chasing an unattainable notion of perfection.

In conclusion, in a world that constantly pushes for perfection, it is essential to let go of unrealistic standards. Understand that perfection is an illusion and that everyone has flaws. Embrace your imperfections as they make you unique. Recognize that true beauty lies in authenticity, not in conforming to societal ideals. Challenge the sources of these standards and focus on setting realistic goals for your personal growth. Remember, you are a work in progress, and that is perfectly okay.

Exercise: Letting Go of Unrealistic Standards

Duration: 30 minutes

Unrealistic standards can create unnecessary stress, anxiety, and self-doubt in our lives. It's important to learn how to let go of these standards to promote self-acceptance and overall well-being. This exercise will guide you through a process of identifying and releasing unrealistic standards you may be holding onto. It will help you cultivate self-compassion and embrace a more realistic and balanced approach to life.

Instructions:

1. Find a quiet and comfortable place where you can focus without distractions. Have a pen and paper or a journal nearby.

2. Take a few deep breaths to relax your body and mind. Close your eyes if it helps you to center yourself.

3. Reflect on areas of your life where you tend to set unrealistic standards for yourself. It could be related to work, relationships, physical appearance, achievements, or any other aspect of your life. Allow yourself to become aware of these areas without judgment.

4. Open your eyes and grab a pen and paper. Create two columns: "Unrealistic Standards" and "Realistic Standards."

5. In the "Unrealistic Standards" column, write down the specific expectations or standards you have set for yourself in each area you identified earlier. Be as detailed as possible. For example, if you have set unrealistic standards for your physical appearance, you might write, "I must have a perfect body with no flaws."

6. Once you have listed your unrealistic standards, go through each one and ask yourself the following questions:

A) What evidence do I have that this standard is realistic or achievable?

B) How does holding onto this standard affect my well-being and happiness?

C) What are the negative consequences of not meeting this standard?

7. Now, move to the "Realistic Standards" column. Rewrite each unrealistic standard in a more realistic and balanced way. Focus on setting standards that are achievable and aligned with your values and capabilities. For example, in the previous example, you might write, "I will strive to take care of my body through healthy habits, but I accept that it will have imperfections."

8. Take a moment to reflect on the new realistic standards you have set. Notice how they feel compared to the unrealistic ones. Embrace the idea that these realistic standards are healthier and more compassionate towards you.

9. Finally, make a commitment to practicing self-compassion and embracing these realistic standards moving forward. Remind yourself that you are human and that it's okay to have flaws and make mistakes. Focus on progress rather than perfection.

2.2 Embracing Flaws as Unique Features

Flaws are not something to be ashamed of; they are unique features that contribute to our individuality and make us who we are. Rather than hiding or denying our flaws, it is essential to embrace them wholeheartedly. By doing so, we not only cultivate self-compassion but also build a healthier and more authentic relationship with ourselves. Embracing our flaws allows us to develop a deeper sense of self-acceptance and understanding. It is through acknowledging our imperfections that we can truly begin to appreciate and love ourselves unconditionally. Instead of perceiving flaws as negative aspects of our being, we can view them as opportunities for personal growth and transformation. Taking the time to reflect on our flaws can be a powerful exercise in self-discovery. By examining our shortcomings, we gain insight into our strengths and weaknesses. We may uncover hidden talents, develop new skills, or find innovative ways to overcome challenges. Our flaws can serve as reminders of the resilience, strength, and perseverance we possess.

Moreover, our flaws often contribute to our uniqueness and make us more relatable to others. They can be the quirks in our personalities that make us interesting, endearing, and memorable. When we embrace these imperfections, we allow others to see us as authentic human beings, flaws and all. This vulnerability can foster deeper connections and meaningful relationships.

It is important to shift our perspective and let go of the societal pressure to be flawless. Nobody is perfect, and striving for flawlessness is an unrealistic and exhausting pursuit. Instead, we should celebrate our imperfections and recognize that they are an integral part of our identity. Our flaws add depth, character, and color to our lives. By accepting and embracing our flaws, we liberate ourselves from the need for external validation. We no longer seek approval or validation from others because we have learned to validate and accept ourselves. This newfound self-acceptance brings a sense of contentment and inner peace. In essence, embracing our flaws is an act of self-love. It is a journey towards wholeness and authenticity. By celebrating our uniqueness, we can fully embrace our beautifully imperfect selves and live a life guided by self-compassion, growth, and self-acceptance. So, let us embrace our flaws, for they are the threads that weave the tapestry of our lives.

Exercise: Embracing Flaws as Unique Features

Duration: 20-30 minutes

Materials needed: Pen/pencil, paper, and a mirror.

Embracing our flaws and unique features is an essential part of cultivating self-acceptance and building confidence. This exercise aims to help you recognize and appreciate your perceived flaws as distinct and beautiful aspects of your individuality.

Instructions:

1. Reflect on your perceived flaws:

Take a few moments to think about the aspects of yourself that you consider flaws or imperfections. It could be a physical feature, a personality trait, or something else that you often criticize about yourself.

2. Write a list of your perceived flaws:

Grab a pen and paper and create a list of the flaws you identified in the previous step. Write each flaw down as a separate point on the list.

3. Challenge your perspective.

For each flaw you listed, try to reframe it in a positive light. Consider how this flaw might contribute positively to your life or make you unique. Write down a positive reinterpretation of each flaw.

For example:

Flaw: Crooked nose

Positive reinterpretation: My crooked nose adds character to my face and makes me stand out from the crowd.

4. Embrace your flaws through self-affirmation:

Stand in front of a mirror, if available, and look at yourself. Take a deep breath and repeat the following affirmations aloud or in your mind:

- I accept and love myself as I am, flaws and all.
- My flaws are unique features that make me who I am.
- I am beautiful/handsome and worthy, regardless of any perceived flaws.

Repeat these affirmations several times, allowing yourself to internalize the positive messages.

5. Celebrate your flaws creatively.

Take out your pen and paper again, and this time, think of a creative way to celebrate and showcase one of your flaws. It could be through drawing, writing, or any other artistic expression that resonates with you. Let your imagination flow and allow yourself to see the beauty in your flaws as you create.

6. Reflect on your experience.

Take a moment to reflect on the exercise. How did it feel to reframe your flaws in a positive light? Did you discover anything new about yourself or gain a different perspective on your flaws? Write down your reflections in your journal or on a separate piece of paper.

Remember that embracing your flaws is an ongoing journey. By recognizing and celebrating your unique features, you can build self-acceptance and foster a positive self-image. Regularly revisit this exercise and continue to explore new ways to embrace and love yourself just as you are.

2.3 Celebrating the Beauty of Diversity

Diversity is a fundamental aspect of our world, permeating every corner of our existence. It encompasses more than just physical appearances; it encompasses a vast array of characteristics, experiences, backgrounds, and perspectives that make each person unique. By celebrating diversity, we acknowledge and appreciate the beauty that arises from our differences.

In today's interconnected and globalized world, the importance of recognizing and celebrating diversity cannot be overstated. It is through diversity that we gain a deeper understanding of the human experience and broaden our horizons. It allows us to break free from narrow-mindedness and embrace the richness that comes from encountering different cultures, beliefs, and ways of life. Accepting imperfections is an integral part of celebrating diversity. It means acknowledging that there is no singular definition of beauty or perfection. By recognizing that beauty lies in the vast array of human experiences and expressions, we can move away from unrealistic standards and embrace the authenticity of our individual and collective imperfections.

Expanding our understanding of beauty requires actively engaging with diverse cultures, beliefs, and perspectives. By exposing ourselves to different ways of thinking and living, we gain a more comprehensive view of the world. We can read books, watch films, visit museums, and attend cultural events that showcase the diversity of human creativity and expression. These experiences allow us to challenge our assumptions and preconceived notions about what is considered "normal" or "ideal."

Engaging in conversations with people who have diverse backgrounds and perspectives is another powerful way to celebrate diversity. By actively listening and empathizing with others, we can gain insights into their unique experiences and broaden our own understanding. These conversations enable us to challenge our biases, expand our perspectives, and cultivate a deeper sense of empathy and compassion. Embracing diversity also means recognizing and addressing systemic inequalities and barriers that hinder the full participation of certain individuals or groups in society. It requires actively advocating for equal opportunities, social justice, and inclusivity. By amplifying marginalized voices and promoting diversity in leadership positions, we can create spaces where everyone's contributions are valued and respected.

When we accept imperfections and celebrate diversity, we foster a more inclusive and compassionate society. We create an environment where everyone, regardless of their differences, feels seen, heard, and valued. By embracing diversity, we not only enrich our own lives, but also contribute to the greater good of humanity. It is important to note that celebrating diversity is not a one-time event or a mere slogan. It is an ongoing and continuous journey that requires self-reflection, education, and active engagement. It requires a commitment to challenging our own biases and dismantling systems of oppression. By embracing diversity, we can create a world that embraces the inherent worth and dignity of every individual, and where the beauty of our collective imperfections shines brightly.

3

NURTURING SELF-CARE PRACTICES

"Self-care is not a luxury, but a vital practice that nourishes our well-being. In nurturing ourselves, we cultivate the strength and resilience needed to thrive in every aspect of our lives." - **Chanelle Fleary**

In the relentless and fast-paced world we find ourselves in, it has become increasingly crucial to prioritize self-care as an integral aspect of maintaining our overall well-being. This pivotal chapter embarks on an exploration of various strategies and approaches aimed at cultivating and nurturing self-care practices, which in turn serve to enhance our physical, mental, and emotional health. Amidst the demands, pressures, and responsibilities that often consume our daily lives, taking the time to invest in ourselves becomes an essential means of preserving and replenishing our inner resources. Recognizing the significance of self-care as a fundamental pillar of personal growth and fulfillment, this chapter offers valuable insights and practical guidance to empower individuals on their journey towards optimal well-being. Within these pages, readers will be introduced to a spectrum of self-care rituals that extend beyond the traditional notion of indulging in occasional treats or pampering sessions. Instead, the focus lies on cultivating sustainable and meaningful practices that integrate seamlessly into our daily routines, fostering a holistic approach to self-care that permeates all aspects of our lives. From prioritizing physical health through regular exercise, nourishing nutrition, and adequate rest, to nurturing mental well-being through mindfulness, stress management, and cognitive exercises, this chapter provides a comprehensive roadmap for individuals seeking to establish a solid foundation of self-care. Furthermore, it explores the profound impact of emotional self-care, emphasizing the importance of self-reflection, emotional intelligence, and fostering healthy relationships as integral components of our overall well-being. By delving into the multifaceted nature of self-care, this chapter encourages readers to embrace self-compassion, self-awareness, and self-empowerment as they embark on their personal journey towards enhanced well-being. It serves as a reminder that self-care is not an indulgence or a luxury; rather, it is an essential investment in ourselves that fuels our ability to navigate life's challenges, cultivate resilience, and ultimately lead a more fulfilling and balanced existence.

By nurturing self-care practices, individuals can embark on a transformative path towards holistic well-being, enabling them to thrive amidst the complexities of modern existence while prioritizing their own health, happiness, and fulfillment.

3.1 Prioritizing Rest and Relaxation

In our modern era characterized by a relentless pace and ever-increasing demands, it has become increasingly crucial to recognize the paramount importance of prioritizing rest and relaxation as integral parts of our self-care practices. Amidst the perpetual hustle and bustle, it is easy to overlook the significance of carving out time for restful activities. However, doing so not only holds the power to rejuvenate our bodies but also plays a transformative role in replenishing our mental and emotional well-being.

Rest and relaxation serve as vital antidotes to the overwhelming stress and pressures that we encounter on a daily basis. In a world where productivity is often celebrated at the expense of personal well-being, we must actively counterbalance this narrative by embracing the value of rest. It is during periods of rest that our bodies have the opportunity to repair and recharge, allowing us to function optimally in all aspects of our lives.

Beyond the physical benefits, rest and relaxation offer profound advantages for our mental and emotional state. Engaging in activities that induce relaxation, such as meditation, deep breathing exercises, or immersing ourselves in nature, affords us moments of respite from the incessant chatter of our minds. By intentionally creating space for stillness, we enable ourselves to cultivate a sense of calm and tranquility. This, in turn, supports greater mental clarity, enhanced focus, and improved overall cognitive function.

Moreover, rest and relaxation provide a nourishing balm to our emotional well-being. When we allow ourselves to step away from the relentless demands of our daily lives, we create an opportunity to reconnect with our inner selves. By engaging in activities that bring us joy and pleasure, whether it be reading a book, indulging in a hobby, or spending quality time with loved ones, we foster a sense of emotional rejuvenation. This, in turn, equips us with the emotional resilience and capacity to navigate life's challenges with greater ease and grace.

In essence, prioritizing rest and relaxation is not a luxury but a vital necessity in our fast-paced and demanding world. By recognizing their transformative power, we empower ourselves to lead lives that are more balanced, fulfilling, and sustainable. So, let us carve out intentional moments of rest, embrace activities that bring us solace and joy, and cultivate a deeper connection with ourselves. In doing so, we embark on a journey of self-care that enriches every facet of our being, ensuring our physical, mental, and emotional well-being thrives in harmony with the demands of our modern lives.

Exercise:

1. Establish a Sleep Routine: Create a consistent sleep schedule by going to bed and waking up at the same time each day. Make your sleep environment comfortable, dark, and quiet to promote quality sleep.

2. Practice Relaxation Techniques: Incorporate relaxation techniques such as deep breathing exercises, meditation, or mindfulness into your daily routine. These practices can help calm your mind and reduce stress.

3. Unplug and disconnect: Take regular breaks from technology and disconnect from work-related activities. Engage in activities that help you unwind, such as reading a book, taking a bath, or spending time in nature.

4. Schedule Downtime: Block off time in your schedule specifically for rest and relaxation. Treat it as an important appointment and prioritize it as you would any other commitment.

5. Engage in Hobbies: Pursue activities that bring you joy and help you unwind. Whether it's painting, gardening, playing an instrument, or cooking, find activities that allow you to disconnect from stress and focus on something you enjoy.

3.2 Engaging in Mindful Eating Habits

Mindful eating is a transformative practice that goes beyond simply consuming food. It involves a deliberate and conscious approach to the act of eating, where one pays full attention to the present moment and engages in a deep awareness of the entire eating experience.

By practicing mindful eating, individuals develop a heightened sense of their body's cues, such as hunger and fullness, as well as the taste, texture, and aroma of the food they consume. It encourages a non-judgmental and compassionate attitude towards oneself and the food choices made.

This practice offers numerous benefits, both physically and mentally. On a physical level, mindful eating promotes healthier eating habits by helping individuals recognize and respond to their bodies' actual nutritional needs rather than emotional or external triggers. It cultivates a more attuned relationship with food, allowing for a greater understanding of the body's hunger and satiety signals.

Furthermore, mindful eating can contribute to weight management by reducing overeating and mindless snacking. It encourages enjoyment and appreciation of food, leading to a more balanced and satisfying eating experience. By savoring each bite and fully engaging the senses, individuals derive more pleasure and fulfillment from their meals.

On a mental and emotional level, mindful eating promotes a sense of mindfulness and presence. It helps individuals become more attuned to their thoughts, feelings, and sensations during mealtime, fostering a deeper connection with their bodies and their overall well-being. It encourages individuals to slow down and create a space for self-care, allowing them to nourish not only their bodies but also their minds.

Moreover, practicing mindful eating can help individuals develop a healthier relationship with food and their body image. It promotes self-acceptance, self-compassion, and a non-judgmental attitude towards food choices. By letting go of restrictive or guilt-inducing thoughts around eating, individuals can embrace a more balanced and positive approach to nourishing themselves.

In summary, mindful eating is a powerful self-care practice that invites individuals to be fully present and attentive to their eating experience. By cultivating awareness, non-judgment, and a deep connection with food, individuals can develop healthier eating habits, nourish their bodies and minds, and foster a positive relationship with food.

Exercise:

1. Slow down: Eat slowly and savor each bite. Pay attention to the taste, texture, and aroma of the food. By eating mindfully, you can better recognize when you feel satisfied and avoid overeating.

2. Listen to Your Body: Tune into your body's hunger and fullness signals. Eat when you are hungry and stop when you are comfortably satisfied. Learn to differentiate between physical hunger and emotional hunger.

3. Eliminate distractions: Minimize distractions while eating, such as watching TV or working on your computer. Instead, create a calm and peaceful environment that allows you to focus on your meal.

4. Choose Nutrient-Dense Foods: Prioritize foods that are nourishing and provide your body with essential nutrients. Include a variety of fruits, vegetables, whole grains, lean proteins, and healthy fats in your meals.

5. Practice gratitude: Cultivate gratitude for the food you are consuming. Take a moment to appreciate the effort that went into growing, preparing, and serving the meal. This can enhance your enjoyment and connection with your food.

3.3 Finding Joy in Movement and Exercise

Participating in regular physical activity offers a multitude of benefits that extend beyond the realm of physical health. Not only does it contribute to our overall well-being, but it also plays a significant role in enhancing our mental and emotional states.

Engaging in joyful movement and exercise has been proven to have a positive impact on our mood. When we exercise, our bodies release endorphins, often referred to as "feel-good" hormones, which can induce feelings of happiness and euphoria. This natural mood booster can help alleviate symptoms of depression, anxiety, and stress, providing a much-needed mental and emotional lift.

Moreover, physical activity serves as an effective stress reliever. When we engage in exercise, our bodies release tension and accumulated stress, allowing us to experience a sense of relaxation and tranquility. It acts as a healthy outlet for negative emotions, channeling our energy into something productive and positive. Regular exercise can also improve sleep quality, which in turn positively affects our mental well-being, leaving us feeling refreshed and rejuvenated.

In addition to its psychological benefits, regular physical activity can also boost our energy levels. While it may seem counterintuitive, spending energy through exercise actually increases our overall energy and stamina. By improving cardiovascular health and increasing blood flow, exercise enhances oxygen and nutrient delivery to our muscles and tissues, resulting in increased vitality and improved cognitive function.

Furthermore, engaging in physical activity can have a profound impact on our overall quality of life. By investing time and effort in maintaining an active lifestyle, we enhance our physical capabilities, allowing us to perform daily tasks with greater ease and efficiency. This increased physical fitness can lead to improved self-esteem, body image, and self-confidence, which can have a positive ripple effect on our mental and emotional well-being.

Regular physical activity offers a wide range of benefits that extend far beyond physical health. By incorporating joyful movement and exercise into our lives, we can experience improved mood, reduced stress levels, increased energy, and an overall enhanced quality of life. Prioritizing our mental and emotional well-being alongside our physical health is crucial for achieving optimal overall well-being.

Exercise:

1. Explore Different Activities: Find physical activities that you genuinely enjoy. It could be dancing, hiking, swimming, cycling, yoga, or any other form of exercise that brings you pleasure. Experiment with different activities until you find what resonates with you.

2. Set Realistic Goals: Set realistic goals that align with your abilities and interests. Avoid focusing solely on outcomes like weight loss or muscle gain. Instead, set goals that emphasize how you want to feel during and after exercise, such as increased energy or a sense of accomplishment.

3. Make it fun: Inject fun into your exercise routine by incorporating elements that bring you joy. Listen to your favorite music or podcasts while working out, exercise with a friend or join group classes that create a supportive and enjoyable environment.

4. Practice mindful movement: Pay attention to your body and how it feels during exercise. Focus on the sensations, the rhythm of your breath, and the movements you're making. This mindfulness can help you stay present and fully engage in the activity.

5. Embrace Variety and Flexibility: Avoid getting stuck in a monotonous exercise routine. Mix up your activities to keep them exciting and prevent boredom. Try new classes, explore different outdoor environments, or incorporate strength training, cardio, and flexibility exercises into your routine.

6. Practice Self-Compassion: Be kind and compassionate toward yourself when it comes to exercise. Listen to your body's needs and honor them. If you're feeling tired or need a break, allow yourself to rest without guilt or judgment.

7. Celebrate Progress: Acknowledge and celebrate your progress, no matter how small. Recognize the positive changes that exercise brings to your overall well-being, such as increased stamina, improved mood, or better sleep quality.

Self-care is an incredibly significant and deeply personal journey that we must embark on in order to nurture our overall well-being and cultivate a balanced and fulfilling life. It is important to recognize that self-care practices will differ from person to person, as we all have unique needs, preferences, and circumstances. Therefore, it is essential to explore and discover self-care rituals that truly resonate with us individually.

One vital aspect of self-care is prioritizing rest and relaxation. In our fast-paced and demanding world, taking the time to rest and recharge is crucial for our mental, emotional, and physical health. This could mean setting aside dedicated downtime, engaging in activities that help us unwind, or simply allowing ourselves to pause and recharge whenever needed. By honoring our need for rest, we create space for rejuvenation and replenishment, which ultimately enhances our overall well-being.

Mindful eating habits are another important facet of self-care. Nourishing our bodies with wholesome and nutritious foods not only supports our physical health but also contributes to our mental and emotional well-being. Mindful eating involves paying attention to our bodies' hunger and fullness cues, savoring each bite, and choosing foods that nourish and energize us. By cultivating a positive and mindful relationship with food, we can enhance our overall well-being and establish a healthier and more balanced approach to nutrition.

Additionally, finding joy in movement and exercise is a powerful way to care for ourselves. Engaging in physical activities that bring us happiness and fulfillment not only benefits our physical health but also has a profound impact on our mental and emotional well-being. Whether it's dancing, hiking, practicing yoga, or participating in team sports, finding activities that we genuinely enjoy encourages us to stay active, boosts our energy levels, and promotes a positive mindset. Movement and exercise not only contribute to our physical fitness but also serve as a powerful tools for stress reduction, improving mood, and fostering a sense of overall well-being.

Ultimately, self-care is a multifaceted and dynamic journey that requires us to be attuned to our own needs, preferences, and desires. By prioritizing rest and relaxation, practicing mindful eating habits, and embracing joyful movement and exercise, we can nurture our well-being on multiple levels and create a life that is fulfilling, balanced, and harmonious. Remember, self-care is not a luxury but a necessity, and investing in our own well-being allows us to show up as our best selves in every aspect of our lives.

4

HEALING AND FORGIVING

"Healing begins when we have the courage to face our pain, and forgiveness is the key that unlocks the door to true liberation. By embracing both, we empower ourselves to create a future filled with love, compassion, and inner peace." - Chanelle Fleary

The Healing Power Within:

Healing is a multifaceted process that encompasses the physical, emotional, and spiritual aspects of our being. It begins with acknowledging the pain we carry within us and allowing ourselves to feel it without judgment. By embracing our vulnerability, we create a safe space for healing to unfold. Through self-compassion, self-care, and seeking support, we tap into the innate healing power that resides within each of us. We learn to listen to the whispers of our bodies, nurturing them with love and tenderness as we embark on a journey of restoration.

Unraveling the Chains of Resentment:

Forgiveness is often misunderstood, as it is not a condoning of past actions but rather a liberation from the burdensome weight of resentment. When we hold onto grudges, we inadvertently anchor ourselves to the past, preventing our own growth and healing. Forgiveness is a courageous act of self-liberation, where we release the grip of bitterness and resentment, allowing space for healing and renewal. It is a transformative process that invites us to let go, find compassion for ourselves and others, and free our hearts from the shackles of pain.

Embracing Self-Forgiveness:

In the midst of our journey, we often discover the need for self-forgiveness. We may carry guilt, shame, or regret for past actions or perceived shortcomings. However, true healing necessitates extending forgiveness towards ourselves. By acknowledging our humanness and embracing self-compassion, we create an environment of acceptance and growth. Self-forgiveness is an act of self-love, granting us permission to move forward, unburdened by the weight of self-judgment, and embracing the beauty of our imperfections.

The Dance of Healing and Forgiving:

Healing and forgiving are intertwined, each nurturing and supporting the other. As we embark on the path of healing, forgiveness becomes an integral part of our journey, and vice versa. As we heal, we find the strength to forgive, and through forgiveness, we discover the key to profound healing. The dance between healing and forgiving is a delicate yet empowering process that allows us to reclaim our bodies, minds, and spirits.

"To My Body With Love" is an ode to the power of healing and forgiveness. It reminds us that our bodies hold the capacity for profound transformation, resilience, and self-love. Through the journey of healing, we learn to embrace our wounds as part of our unique narrative, and through forgiveness, we discover the freedom to create a brighter future. May this chapter serve as a guiding light on your path to healing and forgiveness, igniting the flame of self-love within your heart and soul.

Exercise: Cultivating Forgiveness and Healing

Instructions:

Find a quiet and comfortable space where you can engage in self-reflection without distractions. Take a few moments to ground yourself by focusing on your breath, allowing it to flow in and out naturally. When you feel centered, begin the exercise.

Step 1: Reflect on Past Wounds

Close your eyes and bring to mind a past experience or person that has caused you pain or hurt. Allow yourself to fully acknowledge and feel the emotions that arise. Without judgment, explore the impact it has had on your life, both physically and emotionally. Take your time to delve into the depths of this experience, acknowledging any lingering resentment or anger.

Step 2: Release through writing.

Grab a pen and paper or open a blank document on your computer. Begin writing a letter to yourself or to the person who has caused you pain. Pour your heart out onto the pages, expressing your emotions, thoughts, and desires for healing and forgiveness. Be honest and vulnerable, allowing the words to flow freely without self-censorship. Write as if you are having a heartfelt conversation with yourself or the person involved.

Step 3: Practice Compassion

Once you have finished writing, take a moment to read through your letter. As you do, shift your perspective from anger or resentment to one of compassion and understanding. Imagine the person who caused you pain as a flawed human being, capable of making mistakes and carrying their own burdens. Seek empathy for their journey and the circumstances that may have contributed to their actions.

Step 4: Offer forgiveness.

In your letter, consciously choose to forgive. Write down your intentions for releasing the pain and resentment you have been carrying. Acknowledge that forgiveness is a gift you give yourself, freeing your heart and mind from the weight of the past. Embrace the healing power of forgiveness as an act of self-love and personal growth.

Step 5: Ritual of Release

After completing your letter, take a moment to hold it in your hands. Visualize the pain and resentment being transferred to the paper. When you are ready, you may choose to burn the letter, symbolizing the release of negative emotions and the beginning of the healing process. Alternatively, you can tear the letter into small pieces and discard them as a representation of letting go.

Step 6: Self-Care and Healing Ritual

Engage in an act of self-care that promotes healing and self-love. It could be taking a relaxing bath, practicing meditation or mindfulness, engaging in a creative activity, or spending time in nature. Allow yourself to fully embrace this moment of nurturing and restoration, knowing that you have taken a significant step towards forgiveness and healing.

Remember, forgiveness and healing are ongoing processes that require patience and self-compassion. Repeat this exercise as often as needed, adapting it to suit your unique circumstances and needs. Embrace the power of forgiveness and healing to create a brighter and more compassionate relationship with yourself and others.

4.1 Releasing Past Traumas and Negative Body Experiences

Healing is a profound and transformative journey that involves acknowledging, addressing, and ultimately releasing past traumas and negative body experiences. These experiences have the potential to inflict deep wounds that can permeate every aspect of our being, affecting our emotional, mental, and physical well-being. In order to embark on the path of healing, it is essential to recognize and release the hold these traumas have on us. One powerful and effective means of releasing past traumas is through therapy. Seeking the guidance of a trained professional provides a safe and supportive space to explore and process these experiences. In therapy, we can gain invaluable insights into the root causes of our pain, unravel the complex layers of our trauma, and develop coping strategies to navigate the challenges that arise. Through therapeutic interventions, we can also learn techniques to reframe our perspectives, enabling us to view ourselves and our experiences in a more empowering and healing light. Therapy allows us to confront our traumas head-on, express our emotions, and gradually let go of the heavy emotional and psychological burden they carry in our lives.

Additionally, practices such as mindfulness and meditation can be instrumental in releasing past traumas. By cultivating a state of present-moment awareness and self-observation, we can create a space of non-judgmental acceptance of our thoughts, emotions, and bodily sensations. Mindfulness and meditation provide us with the tools to observe our internal experiences without getting caught up in them, allowing us to develop a deeper understanding of the ways in which past traumas continue to affect us. By creating this awareness, we can gradually let go of the grip that these traumas have on our psyche and begin to heal.

Furthermore, engaging in somatic practices can also contribute to the release of past traumas stored in the body. Traumatic experiences often become embodied, leading to physical tension, pain, and discomfort. Somatic practices such as yoga, dance, breathwork, and body-based therapies provide avenues for reconnecting with our bodies, releasing stored tension, and facilitating the integration of past traumas. These practices allow us to engage with our bodies in a nurturing and compassionate way, fostering a sense of safety and empowerment that supports the healing process. The journey to healing involves acknowledging and addressing past traumas and negative body experiences. Through therapy, coaching, mindfulness, meditation, and somatic practices, we can release the hold that these traumas have on us. By doing so, we create space for profound transformation, emotional liberation, and the restoration of our overall well-being.

Exercise: Cultivating Healing and Forgiveness for Your Body

Instructions:

1. Find a quiet and comfortable space where you can focus on yourself without distractions. You may choose to sit or lie down, whichever feels most relaxing for you.

2. Take a few deep breaths, allowing your body and mind to relax with each exhale. Bring awareness to the present moment and let go of any tension or stress you may be holding onto.

3. Open the "To My Body With Love" book to a random page or select a specific page that resonates with you. Read the passage or affirmation slowly and mindfully, allowing the words to sink in.

4. Reflect on any emotions or thoughts that arise as you read the passage. Notice if there are any judgments or negative beliefs about your body that come up. Be gentle with yourself and offer compassion for any painful emotions that may surface.

5. Begin shifting your focus towards forgiveness and healing. Visualize a soft, golden light surrounding your body, bringing warmth, love, and healing energy. Imagine this light penetrating every cell and fiber of your being, soothing and nourishing you on a deep level.

6. As you continue to visualize this healing light, repeat the following affirmations or create your own personalized affirmations:

- "I forgive my body for any pain or suffering it has experienced."

- "I release any resentment or anger I may have towards my body."

- "I choose to love and accept my body unconditionally."

- "I embrace my body's innate wisdom and capacity for healing."

7. Take a few moments to silently repeat these affirmations, allowing the words to resonate within you. Feel the weight of any burdens or self-judgments gradually lift, making space for forgiveness and self-compassion.

8. Now, bring your attention to any specific areas of your body that may require healing or forgiveness. Visualize these areas bathed in the golden light, allowing it to dissolve any pain, tension, or emotional residue they may hold.

9. As you continue to focus on these areas, offer kind and loving words to yourself. Speak directly to your body, expressing gratitude for its strength, resilience, and the ways it has served you throughout your life.

10. Take a few more deep breaths, feeling a sense of peace and gratitude flowing through your entire being. When you're ready, gently bring your awareness back to the present moment.

11. Journaling and Reflection (optional): After completing the exercise, you may find it helpful to write down any insights, emotions, or shifts in perspective that occurred during the process. Reflect on how this practice of healing and forgiveness can support your ongoing relationship with your body.

4.2 Cultivating Forgiveness for Myself and Others

Forgiveness is a profound and transformative act that holds immense power for both ourselves and others. When we harbor resentment and cling to grudges, it weighs heavily on our hearts and obstructs our personal growth. However, by cultivating forgiveness, we can break free from the chains of the past and forge ahead with a profound sense of peace and acceptance. To begin the journey of forgiveness, we must first acknowledge the pain and suffering that we have experienced. It is essential to validate our emotions and give ourselves permission to feel the full range of our feelings, whether it be anger, sadness, or any other emotions that arise. By honoring our feelings, we create a solid foundation for healing and self-compassion. It is through this process of acknowledging and accepting our pain that we can gradually release its grip on us.

Forgiveness does not imply condoning or justifying the actions of others. It does not mean denying the harm that has been done or pretending that everything is okay. Instead, forgiveness is a choice—a conscious decision—to let go of the negative emotions associated with the past. It is about freeing ourselves from the burden of carrying resentment and grudges, and reclaiming our personal power. By forgiving, we release the power those negative emotions have over us, allowing us to move forward with a renewed sense of inner peace. Forgiveness enables us to break free from the cycle of bitterness and resentment, and redirects our energy towards healing and growth. It does not mean that we forget or ignore what has happened, but it empowers us to transcend the pain and transform it into wisdom and strength. Moreover, forgiveness is not solely for the benefit of others; it is also a gift we give ourselves. When we forgive, we unburden ourselves from the heavy weight of anger and resentment. We create space in our hearts and minds for love, compassion, and joy to flourish. The act of forgiveness allows us to heal, grow, and create a brighter future for ourselves.

In cultivating forgiveness, it is important to be patient and gentle with ourselves. It is a process that takes time, and it may involve setbacks along the way. It requires us to practice self-compassion and extend understanding to ourselves, acknowledging that healing is a journey with its own unique timeline. Ultimately, forgiveness is a profound act of liberation. It is a courageous choice to let go of the past, embrace the present, and create a future filled with peace, acceptance, and personal growth. By cultivating forgiveness, we open ourselves to a life of greater freedom, joy, and authentic connection with ourselves and others.

4.3 Embracing Self-Compassion on the Journey to Healing

Self-compassion is a vital component of the healing process. It involves treating ourselves with kindness, understanding, and acceptance, especially during moments of pain and vulnerability. Embracing self-compassion allows us to create a nurturing environment for healing and fosters a sense of worthiness and self-love. One way to cultivate self-compassion is through self-care practices. Engaging in activities that nourish our body and soul, such as getting enough rest, eating nourishing foods, engaging in physical exercise, and spending time in nature, can help replenish our energy and promote overall well-being. Taking the time to prioritize our needs and engage in activities that bring us joy and relaxation is an act of self-compassion.

Another important aspect of self-compassion is practicing self-acceptance and self-forgiveness. It involves recognizing that we are imperfect beings and embracing ourselves fully, flaws and all. Instead of being self-critical, we can choose to be kind and gentle with ourselves, offering words of encouragement and understanding. This allows us to create a safe space within ourselves where healing can thrive.

Mindfulness is also a powerful tool for cultivating self-compassion. By being present and non-judgmental towards our thoughts and emotions, we can develop a compassionate stance towards ourselves. Mindfulness helps us observe our inner experiences without getting caught up in self-criticism or negative self-talk. It allows us to acknowledge our pain and suffering with kindness and understanding.

Additionally, seeking support from others is an important aspect of self-compassion. Surrounding ourselves with a network of loved ones, friends, or support groups can provide us with a sense of belonging and validation. Sharing our experiences, emotions, and challenges with trusted individuals can help us feel seen, heard, and supported, reinforcing our sense of self-compassion.

On the journey to healing, it is crucial to remember that healing is not a linear process. It requires patience, self-compassion, and the willingness to embrace the ups and downs that come with it. By releasing past traumas, cultivating forgiveness, and embracing self-compassion, we can embark on a transformative journey towards healing and create a life of greater peace, joy, and fulfillment.

5

DEVELOPING A POSITIVE BODY IMAGE

"**Developing a positive body image is a journey of self-acceptance and self-love. When we celebrate the unique beauty and strength of our bodies, we unlock the power to radiate confidence and embrace life's adventures with open arms.**" - **Chanelle Fleary**

Developing a positive body image involves embracing your body's unique qualities, challenging societal beauty standards, and practicing self-compassion. Nurture your body through healthy habits, surround yourself with positive influences, and seek support when needed. Remember, it's a journey that takes time, but focusing on self-acceptance and overall well-being is key.

5.1 Challenging Negative Self-Talk

The journey towards developing a positive body image is an ongoing process that requires patience, self-reflection, and a conscious effort to challenge negative self-talk. Negative self-talk encompasses those detrimental thoughts, beliefs, and inner dialogues that we habitually engage in regarding our bodies. To embark on this transformative journey, it is essential to recognize and acknowledge the power that our thoughts and self-perceptions hold over our overall body image. Negative self-talk often manifests itself as harsh criticisms, comparisons, and unrealistic expectations we impose upon ourselves. These thoughts can stem from societal pressures, media influences, personal experiences, or a combination of various factors.

Challenging negative self-talk involves actively questioning and reframing these destructive thoughts. It requires us to challenge the validity and truthfulness of the negative statements we make about our bodies. This process involves replacing those harmful thoughts with more compassionate, realistic, and empowering ones. One effective strategy is to pay attention to the language we use when talking to ourselves. By consciously choosing words that are kind, supportive, and encouraging, we can gradually shift our internal dialogue towards a more positive and accepting tone. For example, instead of criticizing our imperfections, we can choose to celebrate our uniqueness and focus on our strengths and abilities. Additionally, it is crucial to cultivate self-compassion and practice self-care. This involves treating ourselves with kindness, understanding, and forgiveness. Taking care of our physical and mental well-being through activities such as exercise, nourishing our bodies with healthy foods, engaging in relaxation techniques, and surrounding ourselves with positive influences can contribute to a more positive body image.

Seeking support from trusted friends, family members, or professionals can also be immensely helpful in challenging negative self-talk and fostering a healthy body image. Sharing our struggles, seeking guidance, and receiving validation from others who understand and empathize with our experiences can provide valuable perspectives and encouragement.

Remember, developing a positive body image is a personal and unique journey. It requires consistent effort, self-reflection, and a commitment to self-acceptance. By challenging negative self-talk and replacing it with self-compassion, positive affirmations, and supportive thoughts, we can gradually cultivate a healthier and more positive relationship with our bodies.

Exercise:

1. Recognize negative self-talk: Start by becoming aware of the negative thoughts you have about your body. Notice when you engage in self-criticism or use derogatory language towards yourself.

2. Question your thoughts: Once you recognize negative self-talk, question the validity of those thoughts. Ask yourself if there is evidence to support them or if they are based on societal standards or unrealistic expectations.

3. Replace negative thoughts with positive ones: When you catch yourself engaging in negative self-talk, consciously replace those thoughts with positive and affirming ones. For example, if you find yourself thinking, "I hate my thighs," replace it with, "My body is strong and capable."

4. Practice self-compassion: Treat yourself with kindness and understanding. Instead of beating yourself up over perceived flaws, practice self-compassion and remind yourself that everyone has imperfections.

5. Focus on your strengths: Shift your attention from your perceived flaws to your strengths and positive attributes. Celebrate what your body can do rather than solely focusing on how it looks.

5.2 Surrounding Yourself with Supportive People

Cultivating a positive body image is an intricate journey that can be profoundly impacted by the environment we immerse ourselves in. Surrounding yourself with a supportive network of individuals is undeniably crucial to fostering and nurturing a healthy perception of your own body. When we are enveloped by people who uplift, encourage, and embrace us for who we are, the seeds of self-acceptance and self-love are sown, ultimately blossoming into a positive body image.

The power of a supportive social circle lies in its ability to counteract the societal pressures and unrealistic beauty standards that often plague individuals' minds. In a world where media images are meticulously crafted, airbrushed, and often unattainable, having compassionate and understanding individuals by your side can serve as a sanctuary of authenticity. These individuals celebrate the uniqueness of each person, recognizing that beauty is diverse and extends far beyond superficial appearances.

Surrounding oneself with supportive people creates an atmosphere of acceptance where body positivity flourishes. It fosters a safe space where conversations about self-worth, self-care, and body acceptance can openly take place, free from judgment or comparison. In this nurturing environment, individuals can begin to challenge negative self-perceptions and dismantle the deeply ingrained societal narratives that dictate how one should look, dress, or present themselves.

Moreover, a supportive social circle offers a valuable source of perspective and encouragement during moments of self-doubt or vulnerability. They provide reassurance, reminding us that we are more than our physical appearances and that our worth extends far beyond the confines of our bodies. Through their unwavering support, they help us recognize and appreciate our unique strengths, talents, and qualities that make us who we are.

Surrounding yourself with supportive people not only influences your own body image but also enables you to become a positive influence on others. By embracing and uplifting one another, we create a ripple effect that extends far beyond ourselves. We become agents of change, promoting body positivity and self-acceptance in our wider communities.

In conclusion, the impact of a supportive social circle on developing a positive body image cannot be underestimated. By immersing ourselves in an environment filled with understanding, compassion, and genuine support, we can embark on a transformative journey of self-love, acceptance, and body positivity.

Exercise:

1. Identify supportive individuals: Take note of the people in your life who uplift and support you. These can be friends, family members, or mentors who value you for who you are rather than how you look.

2. Limit exposure to negativity: Minimize contact with people who consistently engage in body shaming, negative self-talk, or promote unrealistic beauty standards. Surround yourself with individuals who promote body positivity and acceptance.

3. Seek support groups or communities: Join support groups, online communities, or local organizations that focus on body positivity. Connecting with like-minded individuals can provide you with encouragement and a sense of belonging.

4. Communicate your needs: Let your loved ones know about your journey towards a positive body image. Communicate your needs and boundaries, and express how their support can positively impact your self-image.

5.3 Cultivating Self-Acceptance and Self-Love

Nurturing a deep sense of self-acceptance and genuine self-love is a profound and transformative endeavor that entails embarking on an ongoing and ever-evolving process. To truly cultivate these invaluable qualities within ourselves, we must approach them with unwavering patience, persistent effort, and consistent practice. Self-acceptance, in its essence, involves embracing and acknowledging our entire being, including our strengths, weaknesses, flaws, and imperfections. It requires us to let go of harsh self-judgment and replace it with compassion, forgiveness, and understanding. By recognizing and honoring our authentic selves, we create space for personal growth, healing, and self-discovery.

Similarly, self-love is a profound act of reverence and care for ourselves. It encompasses treating ourselves with kindness, respect, and nurturing our physical, emotional, and spiritual well-being. It involves setting healthy boundaries, prioritizing self-care, and engaging in activities that bring us joy and fulfillment. Through self-love, we tap into our inherent worthiness and learn to cultivate a positive and nurturing relationship with ourselves.

However, the journey towards self-acceptance and self-love is not a linear path or a destination to be reached; rather, it is an ongoing process that unfolds over time. It requires commitment, perseverance, and a willingness to confront and overcome internal barriers and limiting beliefs that may hinder our progress. We may encounter setbacks, moments of self-doubt, or old patterns that resurface, but it is through these challenges that we have the opportunity to deepen our self-awareness and strengthen our resolve.

Patience becomes a vital companion on this transformative journey. It reminds us that personal growth and self-discovery are not achieved overnight. It encourages us to be gentle with ourselves, understanding that change takes time and that it is okay to stumble along the way. Through patience, we cultivate resilience and allow ourselves the space to learn, evolve, and embrace our unique journey of self-acceptance and self-love.

Practice, too, plays a fundamental role in this process. Just as we would develop any skill or cultivate a new habit, self-acceptance, and self-love require consistent effort and conscious action. Engaging in practices such as mindfulness, self-reflection, journaling, affirmations, or seeking support from therapists or support groups can help us deepen our understanding of ourselves, challenge negative self-talk, and nurture a more loving and accepting relationship with ourselves.

In conclusion, the journey of cultivating self-acceptance and self-love is a profound and ongoing process that demands patience, practice, and a commitment to our own well-being. It is a transformative endeavor that allows us to embrace our authentic selves, foster personal growth, and live a life rooted in compassion, fulfillment, and authenticity.

Activities:

1. Practice gratitude: Focus on what you appreciate about your body and overall well-being. Take time each day to reflect on the things your body allows you to do, such as movement, senses, and experiences.

2. Engage in self-care: Prioritize self-care activities that make you feel good about yourself. This can include exercise, nourishing your body with healthy foods, getting enough sleep, and engaging in activities that bring you joy and relaxation.

3. Challenge beauty ideals: Recognize that beauty comes in diverse forms and is not limited to societal standards. Challenge the narrow definitions of beauty by exposing yourself to a wide range of body shapes, sizes, and representations in the media.

4. Focus on holistic well-being: Shift your focus from solely appearance-based goals to overall well-being. Prioritize physical and mental health

6

———

CELEBRATING BODY DIVERSITY

"Celebrating body diversity is an ode to the richness and beauty of humanity. Embracing our differences cultivates a world where everybody is seen, valued, and celebrated for the unique story it tells. Let us honor the kaleidoscope of bodies and empower one another to love ourselves fiercely, just as we are." - Chanelle Fleary

Body diversity celebrates the uniqueness of every individual, regardless of their shape, size, or appearance. By challenging beauty standards, fostering self-love, breaking stereotypes, and empowering individuals, we create a more inclusive and accepting society. Embracing body diversity promotes equality, encourages authenticity, and inspires positive change. Let us celebrate and appreciate the beauty in all bodies, promoting a culture of acceptance and self-empowerment.

Exercise: Embracing Your Unique Body

Objective: This exercise is designed to help individuals embrace and appreciate their unique bodies, fostering self-love and acceptance.

appearance and instead recognize and appreciate inherent beauty in all its varied forms. Simultaneously, the media and advertising industries have played a crucial role in reshaping beauty standards. There has been a notable increase in the representation of diverse bodies on mainstream media platforms. Advertising campaigns and fashion editorials have started featuring models of different sizes, shapes, and ethnic backgrounds, showcasing the beauty that exists beyond the previously limited ideals. This shift in representation has not only provided a more realistic and relatable portrayal of beauty but has also allowed individuals to see themselves reflected in the media, fostering a sense of acceptance and empowerment.

Furthermore, the advent of social media and online platforms has provided a powerful tool for challenging traditional beauty standards. People from all walks of life are now able to share their stories, experiences, and perspectives, creating a global community that supports and uplifts individuals who have been marginalized or excluded by conventional beauty norms. These online spaces have become platforms for promoting self-love, body acceptance, and the celebration of diversity, encouraging individuals to embrace their unique beauty and reject societal pressures to conform.

In conclusion, the transformation in perspectives regarding beauty standards in recent years has been remarkable. The restrictive and unattainable ideals of the past have given way to a more inclusive and diverse understanding of beauty. This shift has been driven by the rise of body positivity movements, increased representation of diverse bodies in media and advertising, and the empowering nature of social media platforms. As we continue to challenge and redefine beauty norms, we move towards a society that embraces and celebrates the beauty that exists in every body, regardless of size, shape, or appearance.

6.2 Embracing Different Body Shapes and Sizes

Embracing body diversity is an essential aspect of promoting inclusivity, acceptance, and empowerment for individuals of all shapes and sizes. It involves recognizing and appreciating the natural variation that exists in human bodies, understanding that there is no single "ideal" body type, and celebrating the beauty and validity of each unique form. Every person has a distinct body shape, size, and proportion that is influenced by a combination of genetic factors, lifestyle choices, and personal health. Bodies come in a wide spectrum of shapes, including hourglass, pear, apple, athletic, and many others. Additionally, body sizes can range from petite to plus-size and everything in between. It is important to understand that these differences are not flaws to be corrected or judged, but rather natural variations that contribute to the rich tapestry of human diversity.

Promoting body diversity requires a shift in societal attitudes and norms. It means moving away from the narrow and unrealistic beauty standards that have been perpetuated for decades and embracing the notion that all bodies are worthy of love, respect, and acceptance. It involves challenging the harmful belief that a single body type should be idolized and instead appreciating the unique qualities and characteristics that different bodies possess. One way to promote body diversity is through representation in the media, fashion, and advertising. By featuring individuals with diverse body shapes and sizes on these platforms, we can break down the limited portrayal of beauty and showcase the reality and richness of human bodies. This representation can help individuals feel seen, validated, and represented, fostering a sense of belonging and self-acceptance.

Education and awareness also play a crucial role in promoting body diversity. By providing accurate information about the range of body shapes and sizes, as well as the factors that influence them, we can challenge misconceptions and stereotypes. This knowledge empowers individuals to embrace their own bodies and appreciate the diversity in others. Furthermore, promoting self-acceptance and self-love is essential in the journey towards embracing body diversity. Society often imposes unrealistic expectations and pressures on individuals to conform to a certain body standard, leading to body dissatisfaction and low self-esteem. Encouraging individuals to cultivate a positive body image, practice self-care, and prioritize their overall well-being can help them develop a healthy relationship with their bodies and foster a sense of confidence and self-worth.

In conclusion, embracing different body shapes and sizes is a vital component of celebrating body diversity. It involves recognizing the natural variation in human bodies, appreciating the beauty and validity of each unique form, and challenging societal norms that promote a narrow definition of beauty. By promoting representation, education, and self-acceptance, we can create a world where all individuals feel empowered, included, and valued, regardless of their body shape or size.

Regardless of societal pressures or standards, everyone deserves to feel comfortable and confident in their own bodies. Embracing body diversity is not only a matter of personal empowerment but also a step towards creating a more inclusive and compassionate society. By valuing and celebrating body diversity, we can break down barriers, challenge harmful stereotypes, and promote equal opportunities for individuals of all shapes and sizes. It's about fostering a culture that embraces and respects the uniqueness of each individual, recognizing that beauty transcends conventional ideals and resides in the diversity of human bodies.

As we continue to strive for body diversity, it is crucial to advocate for policy changes that support inclusivity and representation. This can include initiatives such as promoting diverse body types in the fashion industry, implementing body-positive curricula in schools, and ensuring that healthcare services cater to the diverse needs of individuals.

Moreover, promoting body diversity goes beyond the individual level. It requires collective action and a commitment to dismantling systemic biases and discrimination. By challenging harmful narratives and promoting body positivity in all aspects of society, we can create an environment where individuals are not judged or discriminated against based on their appearance, but rather celebrated for their unique qualities and contributions. By embracing body diversity, we are paving the way for a future where all individuals can live authentically and free from body shame or prejudice. It is a journey that requires ongoing education, compassion, and the willingness to challenge our own biases. Ultimately, by celebrating and embracing the diverse range of body shapes and sizes, we can foster a society that values and respects the inherent beauty and worth of every individual.

6.3 Promoting Inclusiveness and Body Acceptance

Promoting inclusivity and body acceptance is crucial to creating a society that celebrates and respects body diversity. Inclusivity means ensuring that everyone, regardless of their body size, shape, or appearance, feels valued and represented. It involves challenging discrimination and prejudice based on physical appearance and recognizing that all bodies are equally worthy of respect and dignity. Body acceptance goes beyond simply tolerating or accommodating different bodies; it involves actively embracing and celebrating them. This can be achieved by promoting positive body image, encouraging self-care practices, and fostering environments that promote self-acceptance and self-love.

Education and awareness play a vital role in promoting inclusivity and body acceptance. By challenging harmful stereotypes and promoting accurate information about body diversity, we can help create a culture that values all bodies. This includes providing resources and support for individuals struggling with body image issues and promoting mental and emotional well-being.

Furthermore, it is important for individuals to engage in self-reflection and challenge their own biases and judgments about body diversity. By cultivating empathy and understanding, we can contribute to a more inclusive and accepting society where everyone feels comfortable and valued, regardless of their body shape or size.

In conclusion, celebrating body diversity involves shifting perspectives on beauty standards, embracing different body shapes and sizes, and promoting inclusivity and body acceptance. By doing so, we can create a more inclusive and empowering environment for all individuals, fostering a culture that appreciates and values the beauty in every body.

7

EMPOWERING OTHERS

"Empowering others is not about giving them power, but about helping them realize the power they already possess within. By lifting each other up, we create a ripple effect of strength, resilience, and endless possibilities. Together, we can ignite the flames of greatness and inspire the world to shine." - Chanelle Fleary**

Empowering others is a transformative process that involves providing individuals with the tools, knowledge, and confidence to take control of their lives and make positive changes. It is about recognizing and nurturing the inherent potential in others and creating an environment where they can flourish and achieve their goals. Empowerment is not about exerting control or imposing one's will on others. Instead, it is a collaborative and inclusive approach that fosters autonomy, self-belief, and personal growth. When we empower others, we enable them to develop their skills, make decisions, and take responsibility for their actions. It is about creating opportunities for individuals to realize their full potential and become active participants in their own lives.

There are several ways to empower others.

1. Encourage autonomy: Allow individuals to make their own decisions and take ownership of their actions. Provide them with the necessary resources and support to pursue their goals independently. By fostering autonomy, you help develop their problem-solving and decision-making abilities.

2. Provide education and training: Education is a powerful tool for empowerment. By offering access to knowledge and skills, you equip individuals with the means to improve their lives and make informed choices. Providing training and educational opportunities can help individuals gain confidence and develop the necessary skills to succeed.

3. Foster a supportive environment: Create a safe and supportive environment where individuals feel valued, respected, and encouraged. Promote open communication, active listening, and constructive feedback. By fostering a sense of belonging and inclusivity, you empower individuals to express their ideas, take risks, and learn from their experiences.

4. Lead by example: Set a positive example through your own actions and behaviors. Demonstrate integrity, resilience, and a commitment to personal growth. By acting as a role model, you inspire and motivate others to strive for their own success.

5. Recognize and celebrate achievements: Acknowledge and celebrate the achievements of others. Offer praise, recognition, and rewards for their efforts and accomplishments. By highlighting their strengths and successes, you boost their self-esteem and confidence.

6. Encourage collaboration and teamwork: Foster a culture of collaboration and teamwork where individuals can work together, share ideas, and support one another. Encouraging collaboration promotes creativity, innovation, and collective problem-solving.

7. Promote self-belief: Help individuals recognize their own worth and capabilities. Encourage them to set ambitious goals and provide support as they work towards achieving them. By instilling a belief in their own abilities, you empower individuals to overcome obstacles and reach their full potential.

Empowering others is not only beneficial to individuals themselves but also to society as a whole. When individuals are empowered, they become active contributors, capable of making positive changes in their communities. By investing in the empowerment of others, we create a ripple effect of growth, resilience, and positive transformation.

7.1 Supporting and Uplifting Those Around Me

The act of empowering others is a transformative journey that starts with extending unwavering support and actively uplifting those who surround you. It encompasses a multifaceted approach aimed at creating a nurturing environment where individuals can thrive and reach their fullest potential. To embark on this path of empowerment, one must first acknowledge the power of support. By lending a helping hand, offering guidance, and demonstrating genuine care, we can instill a sense of confidence and resilience in others. Whether it's through lending an empathetic ear, providing constructive feedback, or simply being present, our support can serve as a catalyst for personal growth and self-belief. Moreover, creating a positive and encouraging atmosphere is crucial to fostering empowerment. When people are surrounded by optimism, enthusiasm, and belief in their abilities, they are more likely to embrace challenges and overcome obstacles. By promoting a culture that celebrates achievements, encourages risk-taking, and embraces diversity, we can nurture a collective spirit of empowerment that transcends individual limitations.

On this journey, it is vital to help individuals realize their potential. Many people are unaware of their own capabilities and may need guidance to unlock their hidden talents. By actively identifying and nurturing strengths, providing mentorship, and offering opportunities for growth, we can empower individuals to discover their unique skills and passions. By encouraging them to explore new horizons and step out of their comfort zones, we enable them to embrace their full potential and make meaningful contributions to their personal and professional lives. It is also important to acknowledge that empowerment goes hand in hand with overcoming challenges. Life is full of obstacles and setbacks, and it is during these moments that people often feel discouraged or lose sight of their goals. By offering unwavering support, providing resources, and helping individuals develop resilience and problem-solving skills, we can empower them to confront challenges head-on, learn from failures, and emerge stronger than ever before. Ultimately, empowering others is a continuous process that requires dedication, empathy, and a genuine commitment to the well-being and growth of those around us. By providing support, creating an uplifting environment, helping individuals realize their potential, and assisting them in overcoming challenges, we can inspire a ripple effect of empowerment that positively impacts individuals, communities, and society as a whole.

- Active Listening: Practice active listening by giving your full attention to others. Show genuine interest in their thoughts, feelings, and experiences. This not only helps them feel heard but also builds trust and strengthens your connection with them.

- Offering Encouragement: Offer words of encouragement and praise to boost someone's confidence. Acknowledge their efforts, achievements, and strengths. Your support can motivate them to push through difficult times and pursue their goals with determination.

- Providing Resources: Identify resources that can help individuals grow and develop. This could include recommending books, courses, workshops, or connecting them with mentors who can provide guidance and support in their areas of interest.

- Acting as a Mentor: Share your knowledge and experiences with others by acting as a mentor. Offer guidance, advice, and feedback to help them navigate their personal and professional challenges. Encourage them to learn from your successes and failures, and provide them with opportunities to develop their skills.

- Creating a Safe Space: Foster an inclusive and safe space where individuals feel comfortable expressing themselves without fear of judgment. Encourage open dialogue and respect diverse perspectives. This enables people to share their ideas, concerns, and aspirations freely, fostering growth and empowerment.

7.2 Advocating for Body Positivity in Society

The body positivity movement is an incredibly significant and impactful movement that has emerged in recent years. Its primary objective is to challenge and dismantle the prevailing societal beauty standards that perpetuate unrealistic and narrow ideals of attractiveness. At its core, body positivity aims to cultivate an environment of acceptance, inclusivity, and self-love for individuals of all body types. Advocating for body positivity involves a multifaceted approach that encompasses various aspects of our culture and social discourse. It entails not only promoting positive body image and self-acceptance on an individual level but also actively working towards creating a broader cultural shift that celebrates diversity and rejects the harmful practice of body shaming.

One of the key aspects of the body positivity movement is the recognition and affirmation of the inherent worth and beauty of all bodies, regardless of their shape, size, or appearance. It challenges the notion that there is a singular "ideal" body type and emphasizes that all bodies are deserving of love, respect, and acceptance. Moreover, body positivity seeks to challenge the damaging impact of societal beauty standards, which often lead to body dissatisfaction, low self-esteem, and unhealthy behaviors such as extreme dieting and excessive exercise. By promoting body positivity, we strive to create a more inclusive and supportive environment where individuals can embrace their bodies and develop a healthier relationship with themselves.

Another crucial element of advocating for body positivity is fostering a culture that celebrates diversity. This means actively promoting representation and inclusivity in the media, fashion industry, and other influential spheres. It involves challenging the underrepresentation of marginalized body types and actively seeking to amplify diverse voices and perspectives.

Furthermore, body positivity involves challenging and critiquing the pervasive nature of body shaming in our society. It encourages individuals to refrain from judging and criticizing others based on their appearance and to instead cultivate empathy, understanding, and kindness towards one another.

By rejecting body shaming, we contribute to a more compassionate and accepting society where everyone feels valued and respected.

In summary, the body positivity movement is an essential force for social change that aims to challenge societal beauty standards, promote acceptance of all body types, celebrate diversity, and reject body shaming. Through advocating for body positivity, we not only empower individuals to embrace their bodies but also work towards creating a more inclusive and compassionate society for everyone.

Embrace Self-Acceptance: Begin by cultivating self-acceptance and developing a positive relationship with your own body. Recognize that beauty comes in all shapes, sizes, and forms. Practice self-care and focus on the aspects of your body that you appreciate, rather than fixating on perceived flaws.

Challenge Stereotypes: Speak out against harmful stereotypes and unrealistic beauty standards that perpetuate body shaming. Encourage conversations that promote body diversity and highlight the importance of inner qualities and achievements over appearance.

Promote Media Literacy: Raise awareness about media manipulation and its impact on body image. Encourage critical thinking when consuming media, and support initiatives that promote inclusive representation in advertising, fashion, and entertainment industries.

Educate Others: Share information and resources about body positivity with your friends, family, and community. Engage in conversations about self-esteem, body image, and the harmful effects of body shaming. Encourage others to challenge their own biases and embrace body diversity.

Support Inclusive Brands and Campaigns: Patronize brands that promote body positivity and inclusivity. Share and amplify campaigns that celebrate diverse bodies and challenge beauty norms. By supporting these initiatives, you contribute to the demand for more inclusive representation in the marketplace.

Embracing Body Positivity: A Step-Step Exercise

Objective: The objective of this exercise is to develop effective strategies and skills for advocating body positivity in society.

Duration: This exercise can be completed in approximately 30 minutes.

Materials Needed: Paper, pens, and a comfortable space for reflection and brainstorming.

Instructions:

1. Self-Reflection (5 minutes):

Take a moment to reflect on your personal journey towards body positivity. Consider your own experiences, challenges, and victories. Ask yourself the following questions and jot down your thoughts:

- What does body positivity mean to you?

- How has society influenced your perception of your own body and others?

- What are some negative impacts of body shame and unrealistic beauty standards?

2. Understanding the Issue (10 minutes):

Educate yourself about body positivity, its importance, and the impacts of body shame. Use reliable sources such as articles, research papers, or videos. Take notes on key points and statistics that resonate with you.

3. Identifying Strategies (10 minutes):

Think about effective strategies for advocating body positivity in society. Consider the following questions and write down your ideas.

- What platforms or channels can you use to raise awareness about body positivity?

- How can you challenge and counteract beauty standards in your personal and social circles?

- Are there any local organizations or initiatives that promote body positivity? How can you support them?

4. Action Plan (5 minutes):

Based on your reflections and ideas, create an action plan to actively advocate for body positivity in society. Write down specific actions you can take individually or collectively, along with a timeline for implementation. Some examples may include:

- Sharing positive body image messages on social media platforms.

- Organizing or participating in body-positive events or workshops.

- Engaging in conversations with friends, family, or colleagues about body positivity.

- Supporting brands and media that promote inclusivity and diversity in their representations.

5. Self-Care and Self-Love (5 minutes):

Remember that advocating for body positivity starts with self-love and self-care. Reflect on ways you can nurture a positive body image within yourself. Write down at least three self-care practices that promote self-acceptance and body positivity.

6. Reflection and commitment:

Take a moment to review your action plan and self-care practices. Reflect on the importance of advocating for body positivity and the impact it can have on individuals and society. Commit to implementing your action plan and prioritizing self-care as you move forward.

Remember, advocating for body positivity is an ongoing process. Stay committed, be kind to yourself and others, and celebrate the beauty of all bodies.

7.3 Inspiring Change and Spreading Love

Embracing the transformative power of inspiring change and spreading love can be instrumental in empowering individuals and communities, ultimately leading to a profound and lasting positive impact on society as a whole.

When we talk about inspiring change, we refer to the ability to ignite a spark within individuals that motivates them to challenge the status quo, break free from limiting beliefs, and strive for progress. By sharing stories of resilience, determination, and success, we can inspire others to pursue their dreams, overcome obstacles, and reach their full potential. Whether it's advocating for social justice, championing environmental sustainability, or promoting equality and inclusivity, inspiring change requires us to be bold, visionary, and committed to making a difference.

Similarly, spreading love acts as a powerful catalyst for positive transformation. Love has the extraordinary ability to dissolve barriers, bridge divides, and foster unity among diverse groups of people. By cultivating empathy, compassion, and understanding, we can create a nurturing and supportive environment where everyone feels valued and accepted. Through acts of kindness, generosity, and unconditional love, we can uplift others and inspire them to do the same, creating a ripple effect that reverberates throughout society.

Empowerment is at the core of these endeavors. When we empower others, we provide them with the tools, resources, and opportunities they need to flourish. By encouraging self-belief, fostering personal growth, and nurturing leadership skills, we enable individuals to become agents of change in their own right. Empowerment not only enhances individual lives but also strengthens communities, as empowered individuals collaborate, innovate, and work together to address societal challenges and create positive change.

The ultimate result of inspiring change and spreading love is the creation of a more harmonious and inclusive society. As individuals become empowered, they are more likely to contribute positively to their communities, making a difference in areas such as education, healthcare, poverty alleviation, and environmental conservation. The collective impact of these individual efforts cultivates a culture of empathy, respect, and social responsibility, leading to a more equitable and sustainable world for present and future generations.

In conclusion, inspiring change and spreading love are transformative forces that have the potential to empower individuals, foster positive societal impact, and create a world where compassion, understanding, and progress thrive. By embracing these powerful approaches, we can contribute to a brighter future for all.

Lead by Example: Be a role model by embodying the values and qualities you wish to see in others. Practice kindness, empathy, and compassion in your interactions with people.

Exercise: "Acts of Kindness Challenge"

Objective: To inspire change and spread love through small acts of kindness.

Duration: 7 days

Instructions:

Day 1:

Reach out to a friend or family member you haven't spoken to in a while and let them know you're thinking of them. Send them a heartfelt message or give them a call to catch up.

Day 2:

Perform a random act of kindness for a stranger. It could be as simple as holding the door open, paying for someone's coffee, or giving a compliment to brighten their day. Take note of their reaction and how it made you feel.

Day 3:

Volunteer your time for a cause you believe in. Find a local charity or organization and offer your assistance. It could be helping in a soup kitchen, participating in a beach cleanup, or tutoring underprivileged children. Reflect on the impact you made and the gratitude you received.

Day 4:

Write a handwritten note or letter to someone who has made a positive impact on your life. Express your gratitude and let them know how much they mean to you. Send it by mail or hand-delivery it if possible.

Day 5:

Spread positivity on social media. Share uplifting quotes, stories, or articles that inspire change and promote love and kindness. Engage with others by commenting on their posts with words of encouragement and support.

Day 6:

Organize a community event or gathering centered around spreading love and kindness. It could be a potluck dinner, a neighborhood clean-up day, or a charity fundraising event. Encourage others to participate and make a positive difference together.

Day 7:

Reflect on your experiences throughout the week. Write in a journal or create a gratitude list, noting the impact your acts of kindness had on others and yourself. Identify how you can continue spreading love and inspiring change in your daily life moving forward.

Remember, the purpose of this exercise is to inspire change and spread love through small acts of kindness. Each act, no matter how small, has the potential to make a significant difference in someone's life. Let the exercise serve as a reminder that we all have the power to create positive change in the world by spreading love and kindness.

AFTERWORD

In conclusion, "To My Body With Love" is more than just a heartfelt message—it is a commitment to self-acceptance, self-care, and self-love. It encapsulates the journey of embracing our bodies as unique and beautiful vessels that deserve kindness, respect, and gratitude.

Throughout life, our bodies may change, and we may face challenges and insecurities along the way. However, this letter serves as a reminder that our bodies are not objects to be criticized or compared; they are the very essence of our being, allowing us to experience the world and all its wonders.

By addressing our bodies with love, we acknowledge their resilience, strength, and capacity for growth. We recognize that imperfections are part of our individuality, and instead of berating ourselves, we choose to celebrate the remarkable ways our bodies carry us through life's ups and downs.

"To My Body With Love" encourages us to nurture our physical, mental, and emotional well-being. It prompts us to listen to our bodies' needs, granting them rest, nourishment, and movement. It reminds us to engage in self-care practices that replenish our spirits and promote a harmonious relationship with ourselves.

Moreover, this letter inspires us to silence the inner critic and replace it with self-compassion and acceptance. It urges us to let go of societal standards and embrace our unique beauty, whatever shape, size, or form it may take. It empowers us to reclaim our worth beyond external appearances and to recognize the inherent value we possess.

"To My Body With Love" is a testament to the transformative power of self-love. It encourages us to cherish every scar, every curve, every freckle, and every line as a testament to our journey, a testament to the stories etched into our very skin. It invites us to celebrate our bodies as allies and partners in life, rather than adversaries to be conquered.

By cultivating a loving relationship with our bodies, we unlock a wellspring of confidence, resilience, and joy. We become advocates for ourselves, spreading the message of body positivity and inspiring others to embark on their own journey of self-love.

So, to my body with love, let us embark on this lifelong voyage together—a journey of self-discovery, acceptance, and celebration. May we continue to honor and cherish the incredible vessel that allows us to navigate the world. May we embrace our bodies as sources of strength, beauty, and wisdom. And may we always remember that we are worthy of love, just as we are.

ACKNOWLEDGEMENT:

I would like to express my heartfelt gratitude to all those who have contributed to the creation of this book, "To My Body with Love." It has been a journey of self-discovery and empowerment, and I am deeply grateful for the support and inspiration I have received along the way.

First and foremost, I thank God for His grace and mercy over me throughout my life. I have had many close encounters with death, but to God be the glory, I am alive. I would like to thank my body, the vessel that has carried me through life's ups and downs. It is through this miraculous entity that I have experienced the world, felt joy and pain, and learned to embrace the beauty of being alive. My body has taught me resilience, strength, and the importance of self-care. Without its unwavering support, this book would not exist.

I extend my heartfelt appreciation to my husband and children, family and friends for their unconditional love and encouragement throughout this writing process. Your belief in me and your unwavering support have been invaluable, and for that, I say thank you.

I extend my sincere thanks to Dwight D. Fleary and Jewel Casimire-Fleary for their exceptional photography in capturing the essence of my body for my

Acknowledgement:

book, "To My Body With Love." Their talent and dedication have brought my vision to life, and their support has been invaluable. I am deeply grateful for their contribution.

To my editor and the publishing team, thank you for your expertise, guidance, and dedication. Your keen insights, constructive feedback, and meticulous attention to detail have transformed this manuscript into something far greater than I could have ever envisioned.

I would like to express my gratitude to the countless authors, poets, and thinkers whose words have inspired and influenced this work. Your wisdom, creativity, and unique perspectives have shaped my understanding of the body and its connection to the world around us. I am humbled by your contributions to the literary world and grateful for the legacy you have left behind.

Finally, I extend my deepest appreciation to the readers of this book. Your curiosity, open-mindedness, and willingness to embark on this journey of self-acceptance and self-love are what make this book meaningful. It is my sincerest hope that "To My Body with Love" serves as a source of inspiration, empowerment, and healing for all those who engage with its pages.

In conclusion, my gratitude knows no bounds. Each person who has played a role in the creation of this book has left an indelible mark on its pages and, by extension, on my heart. Thank you for joining me on this transformative exploration of the body and may we all continue to cultivate love and appreciation for ourselves and the miraculous vessels that carry us through life.

With love and gratitude,

Chanelle Fleary

ABOUT THE AUTHOR

Chanelle Fleary is an accomplished author, intimate coach, and entrepreneur. Born in Trinidad and Tobago, she later moved to Newark, New Jersey. Chanelle is a loving wife and mother, and her experiences have shaped her understanding of love and relationships. Through her platform, Chanelle Intimate Coach, she provides personalized coaching and resources to help individuals and couples deepen their connections. She also owns theirintimacy.com, an online store dedicated to enhancing intimacy in relationships. Chanelle's story is one of resilience and empowerment.

ABOUT THE BOOK

"To My Body With Love" is a heartfelt and empowering book that celebrates the relationship between oneself and one's body. Authored by an acclaimed self-care advocate, it provides a compassionate and inspiring exploration of body positivity, self-acceptance, and holistic well-being. Through a collection of personal anecdotes, reflective exercises, and practical tips, the book guides readers on a transformative journey towards developing a loving and nurturing connection with their bodies. It encourages readers to embrace their unique physicality, appreciate their body's resilience, and cultivate a positive body image. "To My Body With Love" serves as a gentle reminder that self-love and body acceptance are essential components of a healthy and fulfilling life. With its compassionate tone and insightful wisdom, this book is a powerful tool for anyone seeking to foster a more loving relationship with their body and cultivate a deeper sense of self-worth.